ISBN 978-1-5278-8454-0
PIBN 10897983

This book is a reproduction of an important historical work. Forgotten Books uses
state-of-the-art technology to digitally reconstruct the work, preserving the original format
whilst repairing imperfections present in the aged copy. In rare cases, an imperfection in
the original, such as a blemish or missing page, may be replicated in our edition. We do,
however, repair the vast majority of imperfections successfully; any imperfections that
remain are intentionally left to preserve the state of such historical works.

1 MONTH OF
FREE
READING

at

www.ForgottenBooks.com

By purchasing this book you are
eligible for one month membership to
ForgottenBooks.com, giving you
unlimited access to our entire
collection of over 1,000,000 titles via
our web site and mobile apps.

To claim your free month visit:

www.forgottenbooks.com/free897983

English
Français
Deutsche
Italiano
Español
Português

www.forgottenbooks.com

Mythology Photography **Fiction**
Fishing Christianity **Art** Cooking
Essays Buddhism Freemasonry
Medicine **Biology** Music **Ancient**
Egypt Evolution Carpentry Physics
Dance Geology **Mathematics** Fitness
Shakespeare **Folklore** Yoga Marketing
Confidence Immortality Biographies
Poetry **Psychology** Witchcraft
Electronics Chemistry History **Law**
Accounting **Philosophy** Anthropology
Alchemy Drama Quantum Mechanics
Atheism Sexual Health **Ancient History**
Entrepreneurship Languages Sport
Paleontology Needlework Islam
Metaphysics Investment Archaeology
Parenting Statistics Criminology
Motivational

Spiritual Conceits,

Extracted from the Writings of the Fathers, of the Fathers, the Old English Poets, &c.

& Illustrated by

W. Harry Rogers.

LONDON:

Griffith and Farran,

Corner of St. Paul's Churchyard.

MDCCCLXII.

The engraving by Joseph Swain

To the Reader.

The hundred emblems of Christian Life which are comprised in the present volume require a few words of introduction. It appears necessary to explain in what their speciality consists, and in what respects they differ, as a whole, from other collections of emblems which were so plentifully originated during the sirteenth and seventeenth Centuries, and some of which have in recent years been reprinted. The book now offered to the public is an original illustrated compilation, having only such affinity to its predecessors as must needs result·from its being composed of certain emblematical devices with accompanying letter-prefs, the devices and the letter-prefs fo illuftrating each other as to be manifeftly in-feparable.

In the fecond place, the fact that the editor and the artift are the fame perfon is, probably, a novel feature.

In the third place, the emblems have been fo grouped as not to prefent a mélange of ideas affociated by accident, but to give, as far as poffible, one confecutive feries of thoughts, developing Savanarola's comprehenfive fenti-ment, " If there be no enemy, no fight; if no fight, no victory; if no victory, no crown." The fathers of the Church, the nobleft divines of the Middle Ages, and the old English poets, have been preffed into the fervice of one fired and unaffailable idea, which is clenched in the motto, " No Cross, no Crown;" and to this they have been asked to do duty in such wise as out of discordant parts to make one harmonious whole. Thus the text is old, and as true in earthly as in heavenly things; the materials are venerable, but the grouping and the picturing are new.

The series may be roughly divided into eight sections: 1. The Dual Character of all Things. 2. Past, Present, Future. 3. Preparations for Futurity. 4. Vices. 5. Virtues. 6. Facts. 7. Reflections. 8. Results.

The first section, for example, is represented by the first ten emblems. Earth has its counterpart in heaven; the city of Babylon is exchanged for the typical Jerusalem, the robe of earth for the robe of immortality, the tree of death for that of life, the snares of wealth for the wholesomeness of poverty, Nero's diadem in fetters for the crown of glory of St. Paul. And is there not an exchange of the devotion to Mammon for the hope of the great inheritance, of self-dependence for the modesty of infantine trust, of the darkness of paganism for the kind light of Christianity, of the malevolent for the Holy Trinity, of the eternity of death for the eternity of spiritual life?

The second and third sections speak for themselves: then follow devices indicating the hideousness of vice, succeeded by such as, in still more lively colours, depict the charm of its antithesis, the hopefulness of virtue, the " beauty of holiness." The remainder can probably be worked out by the reader, who will find that from first to last the spirit of the book gradually developes the idea of the ultimate triumph of suffering, and the impossibility of sharing the "crown" without first bearing the "cross;" an idea expressed by Macarius in the words, "Let us suffer with those that suffer, and be crucified with those that be crucified, that we may be glorified with those that be glorified."

In conclusion, if, as most prefaces seem to hint, an excuse or reason be wanted for the making of a book, I can only say that I had been reading at leisure some antique writers, and noting therefrom certain pleasant pieces. In reviewing these gems, I chanced upon such as I thought must needs be threaded. If you think slightly of this printed necklace, consider rather the matter than the manner; but let not any clumsiness of setting disparage the beauty of the pearls.

W. H. R.

Contents

Spiritual Conceits.

The Two Cities.

Wo several lovers built two several cities; the love of God buildeth a Jerusalem; the love of the world buildeth a Babylon: let every one inquire of himself what he loveth, and he shall resolve himself, of whence he is a citizen.

St. Augustine.

Set your affection on things above, not on things on the earth.

Colofs. iii. 2.

The Two Robes.

IS she weeping and lamenting who can find leisure to enrobe herself in precious raiment, without considering that robe of Christ which she has lost: and to take to her costly ornaments and elaborate necklaces never weeping at the forfeiting of her divine and heavenly adorning! Naked thou art, though garbed in foreign draperies and silken robes. Studded with gold and pearls and gems, still thou art unsightly, if God's beauty is wanting.

St. Cyprian.

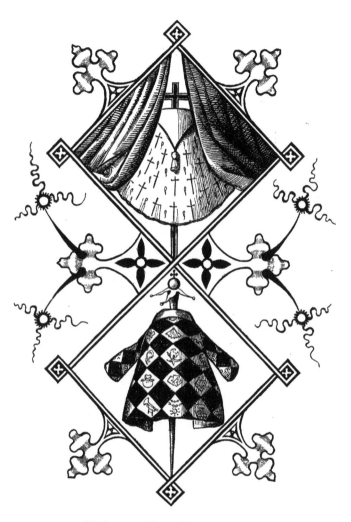

The beauty of holiness. Ps. xxix. 2.
But thou didst trust in thine own beauty. Ezekiel, xvi. 15.

The Two Trees.

O Miferable condition of mankind, that has loft that for which he was created! alas! what hath he loft? and what hath he found? He hath loft happinefs for which he was made, and found mifery for which he was not made.

Anfelm.

A Tree was firft the inftrument of ftrife,
When Eve to fin her foul did proftitute;
A tree is now the inftrument of life.

Giles Fletcher.

God created man to be immortal, and made him to be an image of his own eternity. Nevertheless through envy of the devil came death into the world: and they that do hold of his side do find it.   Wisdom, ii. 23.

The Two Dangers.

Ive us grace to hold a middle course between Scylla and Charybdis, that, both dangers escaped, we may arrive at the port secure.

St. Augustine.

Give me neither poverty nor riches.
Prov. xxx. 8.

The Two Crowns.

Such is the power of Christ. The chain surpassed the kingly crown, and this apparel was shown more brilliant than that. Clothed in filthy rags, as the inhabitant of a prison, he turned all eyes upon the chains that hung on him, rather than on the purple robe.

*   *   *   *

Let us, my beloved children, be imitators of Paul, not in his faith only, but in his life, that we may attain unto heavenly glory, and trample upon that glory that is here.

St. Chrysostom.

The sufferings of this present time are not worthy to be compared with the glory which shall be revealed in us.

Rom. viii. 18.

The Two Choices.

Thou wilt repent
    That for the love of dross, thou hast
      despised
Wisdom's divine embrace; she would have
      borne thee
On the rich wings of immortality;
But now go dwell with cares, and quickly die.

                        Dekker.

There is not a more wicked thing than a covetous man : for such an one setteth his own soul to sale.

Ecclus. x. 9.

The Two Trusts.

They who have built themselves nests in heaven were made helpless and vile outcasts, to the end that being humbled and impoverished, they might learn not to fly with their own wings, but to trust under My feathers.

Thomas à Kempis.

For they learn to trust in the protection of heavenly assistance when they see that many have fallen from their own strength.

St. Gregory the Great.

14

The race is not to the swift, nor the battle to the strong.

Eccles. ix. 11.

The Two Religions.

Can wars and jars and fierce contention,
      Swoln hatred and consuming envy spring
From piety? No, 'tis opinion
That makes the riven heaven with trumpets ring,
And thundering engine murderous balls outfling,
And send men's groaning ghosts to lower shade
Of horrid hell. This the wide world doth bring
To devastation, makes mankind to fade,
Such direful things doth false religion persuade.

But true religion sprung from God above
Is like her fountain, full of charity,
Embracing all things with a tender love,
Full of goodwill and meek expectancy,
Full of true justice and sure verity,
In heart and voice free, large, even, infinite,
Not wedged in strait particularity,
But grasping all in her vast active sprite,
Bright lamp of God, that men would joy in thy
      pure light!

                                        Henry More.

The graven images of their gods ſhall ye burn with fire : thou ſhalt
not deſire the ſilver or gold that is on them, nor take it unto thee, leſt thou
be ſnared therein · for it is an abomination to the Lord thy God.

Deut. vii. 25.

Pure religion and undefiled before God and the Father is this, To viſit
the fatherleſs and widows in their affliction, and to keep himſelf unſpotted
from the world.

James, 1. 27.

The Two Trinities.

Bles'd Father, Son, and Holy Ghost,
　　One God in persons three,
What is there whereof man can boast,
　　Except Thy love it be!

And save this Anti=trinity,
　　The world, the flesh, the devil,
What foe on our humanity
　　Hath power to bring an evil?

　　　　　　　　　G. Wither.

There are Three that bear record in heaven, the Father, the Word, and the Holy Ghost.   1 John, v. 7.

But if ye have bitter envying and strife in your hearts, glory not, and lie not against the truth.   This wisdom descendeth not from above, but is earthly, sensual, devilish.   James, iii. 14, 15.

The Two Eternities.

There are but two ways for this soul to have,
    When parting from the body forth it
    purges,
To fly to Heaven, or fall into the grave,
Where whips of scorpions with the stinging
    scourges
Feed on the howling ghosts, and fiery surges
Of brimstone roll about the cave of night,
Where flames do burn and yet no spark of light,
And fire both fries and freezes the blaspheming
    spright.

                Giles Fletcher.

Some to everlasting life, and some to shame and everlasting contempt.

Daniel, xii. 2.

The Paradox.

O Strange conjunction and alienation; what I fear I embrace, and what I love I am afraid of; before I make war, I am reconciled; before I enjoy peace, I am at variance.

St. Gregory Nazianzen.

With the mind I myself serve the law of God; but with the flesh the law of sin.

Romans, vii. 25.

The Past.

Ane is the golden warld of Assyrians,
   Of whom King Ninus was first and
   principal,
Gane is the silver warld of Persians,
The copper warld of Greekès now is thrall,
The warld of iron, whilk was last of all,
Comparit to the Romans in their glore
Are gane right sae—I hear of them no more.

Sir David Lyndsay.

E came to do away with the old things,
   and to call us to a greater country.

St. Chrysostom.

𝔒𝔩𝔡 things have passed away, and all things have become new.

2 Corinth. v. 17.

The Present.

I Am a little world made cunningly,
Of elements and an angelic spright,
But black sin hath betrayed to endless night
My world's both parts, and oh! both parts must
  die!
You which beyond that heaven which was most
  high
Have found new spheres and of new land can
  write,
Pour new seas in my eyes, that so I might
Drown my world with my weeping earnestly.

       Donne.

We are fearfully and wonderfully made.

Ps. cxxxix. 14.

The Future.

IT must be done, my soul, but 'tis a strange,
  A dismal and mysterious change,
When thou shalt leave this tenement of clay
And to an unknown somewhere wing away,
When time shall be eternity, and thou
Shalt be thou know'st not what, and live thou
      know'st not how.

                              John Norris.

The end of this time and the beginning of the immortality for to come.

2 Esdras, iii. 43.

Pilgrimage.

OUr tears to joy, our fears to faith
Are turnèd, and we see
That our beginning, as one faith,
Shows what our end will be.

John Bunyan.

SEe how great a distance this is to run
over! See how great is the ascent! Thither we must fly up with the wings of the Spirit, otherwise it is impossible to surmount this height. If thou fall, rise up again. Even thus mayest thou obtain the victory.

St. Chrysostom.

We are journeying unto the place of which the Lord said, I will give it you: come thou with us, and we will do thee good · for the Lord hath spoken good concerning Israel.

Numbers, x. 29.

Chrift Afleep.

The fleep of Chrift is a high myftery. The failors are the fouls paffing over the world in wood. That fhip alfo was a figure of the Church. And all individually indeed are temples of God, and his own heart is the veffel in which each fails; nor can he fuffer fhipwreck if his thoughts are only good. Thou haft heard an infult, it is the wind; thou art angry, it is a wave.

St. Auguftine.

And he arofe, and rebuked the wind, and faid unto the fea, Peace, be ftill.

Mark, iv. 39.

Watching.

To good deeds we be sleepy, and to ill awake and watchful. Even Judas Iscariot for the whole night through was wakeful, and he sold the righteous blood that did purchase the whole world. The son of the dark one put on darkness, having stripped the light from off him; and the creator of silver for silver the thief did sell.

St. Ephrem.

See drowsy Peter, see where Judas wakes.

Giles Fletcher.

𝔒 fools! and slow of heart.
          Luke, xxiv. 25.

Swift to shed blood.
          Rom. iii. 15.

The Cup of Babylon.

Babylon is the golden cup." For what is designated by the name of Babylon but the glory of this world? and this cup is said to be golden because while it shows the beauty of temporal things it so intoxicates foolish minds with its concupiscence that they desire temporal display, and despise invisible beauties. For in this golden cup Eve was the first who was made drunken of her own accord, of whom the history of truth says, that when she desired the forbidden tree she saw that it was beautiful to the sight and delightful to the look, and ate thereof. Babylon is therefore a golden cup.

St. Gregory the Great.

Babylon hath been a golden cup in the Lord's hand, that made all the earth drunken: the nations have drunken of her wine; therefore the nations are mad.

Jeremiah, li. 7.

Anger.

IT were good to be silent, good to have no communications with any man in act or word, until we were able to charm the wild beast that is within us. The wild beast, I say, for indeed is it not worse than the attack of any wild beast when wrath and lust make war upon us? Well then do thou first tame thy lion, and so lead him about, not for the purpose of receiving money, but that thou mayest acquire a gain to which there is none equal. For there is nothing equal to gentleness, which both to those that possess it and to those who are its objects is exceeding useful.

St. Chrysostom.

Wrath killeth the foolish man.
Job, v. 2.

Cease from anger, and forsake wrath.
Ps. xxxvii. 8.

Toys.

Life is not a plaything, or rather our pre-sent life is a plaything, but the things to come are not such; or perchance our life is not a plaything only, but even far worse than this. For it ends not in laughter, but rather brings exceeding damage on them who are not minded to order their own ways strictly. For what, I pray thee, is the difference between children who are playing at building houses and us when we are building our fine mansions?

St. Chrysostom.

For what is your life? It is even a vapour, that appeareth for a little
time, and then vanisheth away.

James, iv. 14.

Tyranny of the World.

AGain on the contrary side also we under=
go the same mischief. As wealth is
counted a good thing, and pride, and pomps,
and to be conspicuous: accordingly this again
we pursue, not either in this case from consider=
ing the nature of the thing as good, but persuaded
by the opinion of our masters. For the people
is our master; and the great mob is a savage
master and a severe tyrant; not so much as a
command being needed in order to make us
listen to him; it is enough that we just know
what he wills and without a command we sub=
mit: so great goodwill do we bear towards him.

St. Chrysostom.

The creature was made subject to vanity.

Rom. viii. 20.

Indulgence.

Lᵁₛₜ is a sharp spur to vice, which always putteth the affections in a false gallop.

St. Ambrose.

If I have walked with vanity, or if my foot hath hasted to deceit.

Job, xxxi. 5.

Greed.

He heart is a small thing, but desireth great matters. It is not sufficient for a kite's dinner, and yet the whole world is not sufficient for it.

Hugo.

Ontent thee, greedy heart,
Modest and moderate joys to those that
       have
Title to more hereafter when they part
       Are passing brave.

Geo. Herbert.

For the wicked boasteth of his heart's desire, and blesseth the covetous, whom the Lord abhorreth.

Psalms, x. 3.

Luxury.

Luxury is an enticing pleasure, a bastard mirth, which hath honey in her mouth, gall in her heart, and a sting in her tail.

Hugo.

Withal sweet tastes have four closes,
And he repents in thorns, that sleeps
in beds of roses.

Fra. Quarles.

Scorn delights and live laborious days.

Milton.

Bread of deceit is sweet to a man, but afterwards his mouth
shall be filled with gravel.

Prov. xx. 17.

Hypocrisy.

As are those apples pleasant to the eye,
   But full of smoke within, what used to
     grow
Near that strange lake where God poured from
     the sky
Huge showers of flame worse flames to overthrow,
Such are their works that with a glaring show
Of humble holiness in virtue's dye
Would colour mischief, which within they glow
With coals of sin, tho' none the smoke descry;
But is that angel that erst fell from Heaven
But not so bad as he, nor in worse case,
Who hides a traiterous mind with smiling face,
And with a dove's white feathers clothes a raven;
Each sin some colour has it to adorn,
Hypocrisy Almighty God doth scorn.
William Drummond.

It is a serpent most when most it seems a dove.
Fra. Quarles.

Ye also outwardly appear righteous unto men, but within ye are
full of hypocrisy and iniquity.

Matt. xxiii. 28.

'Bad Fruit.

On, wi seff thou love and herte
 On worldes blisse, that nout ne last?
Wi tholiest thou thin herte smerte
For love that is ounstudefast?
Thou lickest honi of thorn i-wis,
That sett thi love on worldes blis.

MS. temp. Edw. I.

A corrupt tree bringeth forth evil fruit.   A good tree cannot bring forth
evil fruit, neither can a corrupt tree bring forth good fruit.

Matt. vii. 17.

Falsehood.

Who hath not sworn? Yet this thing is of the Evil One. Who hath not forsworn himself? But this man is something more than of the Evil One.

St. Chrysostom.

Love no falfe oath, for all thefe are things that I hate, faith the Lord.

Zech. viii. 17.

Ancestral Pride.

You that but boast your ancestors' proud
      style,
And the large stem whence your vain greatness
      grew,
When you yourselves are ignorant and vile,
Nor glorious thing dare actually pursue,
That all good spirits would utterly exile,
Giving yourselves unto ignoble things,
Base I proclaim you, though derived from kings.

                Michael Drayton.

The divine laws everywhere pronounce
     blessed none of the rich, or of the well-
born, or of the possessors of glory, but those that
have gotten hold of virtue.

              St. Chrysostom.

Then are ye bastards, and not sons.

Heb. xii. 8.

Worldliness.

Behold, the world is withered in itself, yet flourisheth in our hearts, everywhere death, everywhere grief, everywhere desolation: on every side we are smitten; on every side filled with bitterness, and yet with the blind mind of carnal desire we love her bitterness.

St. Gregory.

He hath set the world in their heart.
Eccles. iii. 11.

Deceit of the World.

IN this world is much treachery, little truth; here all things are traps; here everything is beset with snares; here souls are endangered, bodies are afflicted; here all things are vanity and vexation of spirit.

St. Bernard.

As the fishes that are taken in an evil net, and as the birds that are caught in the snare; so are the sons of men snared in an evil time, when it falleth suddenly upon them.

Eccles. ix. 12.

emptation.

HE forced him not: he touched him not: only said, Cast Thyself down; that we may know, that whosoever obeyeth the devil casteth himself down: for the devil may suggest, compel he cannot.

St. Chrysostom.

Which will not hearken to the voice of charmers, charming never fo wifely.

Pſ. lvuı. 5.

# Ambition.

This snatching at a sceptre breaks it: he
    That broken dies ere he can grasp it see:
The poor world seeming like a ball that lights
Betwixt the hands of powerful opposites.

Sir Edward Sherburne.

Thy pomp is brought down to the grave.

Isaiah, xiv. 11.

Vengeance.

'Nor sea, nor shade, nor shield, nor rock,
        nor cave,
Nor silent deserts, nor the sullen grave,
What flame=eyed fury means to smite, can save.

The seas will part, graves open, rocks will split;
The shield will cleave, the frighted shadows flit;
Where Justice aims, her fiery darts must hit.

                        Francis Quarles.

They shall hunt them from every mountain, and from every hill, and
out of the holes of the rocks.   Jer. xvi. 16.

Reflection.

E'En to man's soul, which did God's image
      bear,
And was at first fair, good, and spotless pure,
Since with her sins her beauties blotted were,
Doth of all sights her own sight least endure.

For e'en at first reflection she espies
Such strange chimæras and such monsters there,
Such toys, such antics, and such vanities,
As she retires and shrinks for shame and fear.

                    Sir John Davies.

God hath made man upright; but they have sought out many inventions.

Eccles. vii 29.

The Capture.

IT matters not to the sparrow caught in the snare that he is not held tight in every part, but only by the foot; he is a lost bird for all that; in the snare he is, and it profits him not that he has his wings free, so long as his foot is held tight.

St. Chrysostom.

Whofoever, therefore, ſhall break one of theſe leaſt commandments, and ſhall teach men ſo, he ſhall be called the leaſt in the Kingdom of Heaven.

Matt. v. 19.

Doom.

What! nets and quivers too? what need
    there all
These sly devices to betray poor men?
Die not they fast enough when thousands fall
Before thy dart? what need these engines then?
Attend they not and answer to thy call
Like nightly coveys, where they list and when?
What needs a strategem where strength can
    sway?
Or what needs strength compel where none
    gainsay?
Or what needs strategem or strength, where
    hearts obey?

Francis Quarles.

It is appointed unto men once to die.

Heb. ix. 27.

Evil Passions.

T Is with our mind as with a fertile ground,
    Wanting this love, they must with
    weeds abound,
Unruly passions, whose effects are worse
Than thorns and thistles springing from the
    curse.

Edmund Waller.

For from within, out of the heart of men, proceed evil thoughts, adulteries, fornications, murders, thefts, covetousness, wickedness, deceit, lasciviousness, an evil eye, blasphemy, pride, foolishness.

Mark, vii. 21, 22.

Weeding.

Cultivate thy soul. Cut away the thorns, sow the word of godliness. Nurse with much care the fair plants of Divine Wisdom, and thou hast become a husbandman. Sharpen thy sickle, which thou hast blunted through gluttony.

St. Chrysostom.

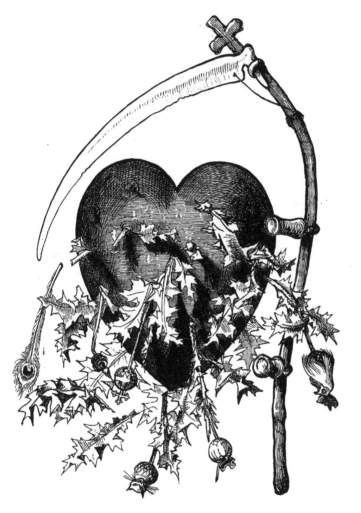

Every plant which My heavenly Father hath not planted shall be rooted up.

Matt. xv. 13.

The Refuge.

TO what place can I safely fly? to what mountain? to what den? to what strong house? what castle shall I hold? what walls shall hold me? whithersoever I go, myself followeth me; for whatsoever thou fliest, O man, thou mayest, but thine own conscience; wheresoever, O Lord, I go, I find Thee: if angry, a Revenger; if appeased, a Redeemer: what way have I but to fly from Thee to Thee! That thou mayest avoid thy God address to thy Lord.

St. Augustine.

In the time of trouble he shall hide me in his pavilion; in the secret of his tabernacle shall he hide me. Ps. xxvii. 5.

Thou art my hiding place. Ps. cxix. 114.

Peace.

But he, her fears to ceafe,
    Sent down the meek-eyed peace;
She, crowned with olive green, came softly
    sliding
Down through the turning sphere, His ready
    harbinger,
With turtle wing the amorous clouds dividing:
And, waving wide her myrtle wand,
She strikes a univerfal peace through fea and
    land.
                   Milton.

Glory to GOD in Highest and on earth PEACE

They shall beat their swords into plowshares, and their spears into pruning-hooks · nation shall not lift up sword against nation, neither shall they learn war any more.

Isaiah, ii. 4.

Regeneration.

'NOw that the Winter's gone, the earth
        hath loſt
Her ſnow=white robes, and now no more the froſt
Candies the graſs, or caſts an icy cream
Upon the ſilver lake or cryſtal ſtream;
But the warm ſun thaws the benumbed earth
And makes it tender, gives a ſacred birth
To the dead ſwallow; wakes in hollow tree
The drowſy cuckoo and the humble bee:
Now do a quire of chirping minſtrels bring
In triumph to the world the youthful Spring.

                        Thomas Carew.

Ye must be born again.
John, iii. 7.

Thirst.

Lord, I thirst, Thou art the Spring of
Life, satisfy me: I thirst, Lord, I thirst
after Thee, the living God!

St. Augustine.

My soul doth thirst to take of Thee a taste,
My soul desires with Thee for to be placed.

Geo. Gascoigne.

As the hart panteth after the water-brooks, so panteth my foul
after Thee, D God.

Ps. xlii. 1.

Iesus.

Welcome, dear, all-adored Name!
  For sure there is no knee
 That knows not Thee;
Or, if there be such sons of shame,
  Alas! what will they do
 When stubborn rocks shall bow,
And hills hang down their heaven-saluting heads,
 To seek for humble beds
Of dust, where in the bashful shades of night,
Next to their own low nothing, they may be,
And couch before the dazzling light of Thy dread
    Majesty!

                        Richard Crashaw.

At the name of Jesus every knee should bow.

Philippians, ii. 10.

The Call.

Ome, my Way, my Truth, my Life,
　　Such a Way as gives us breath,
Such a Truth as ends all strife,
Such a Life as killeth death.

Come, my Light, my Feast, my Strength,
Such a Light as shows a feast,
Such a Feast as ends in length,
Such a Strength as makes his guest.

Come, my Joy, my Love, my Heart,
Such a Joy as none can move,
Such a Love as none can part,
Such a Heart as joys in love.

G. Herbert.

I am the Way, the Truth, and the Life.

John, xiv. 6.

The Lamb.

The Shepherd.

Thomalin.

O Blessed Sheep! O Shepherd Great!
That bought His flock so dear,
And did them save with bloody sweat
From wolves that would them tear.

Spenser.

Behold the Lamb of God, which taketh away the sin of the world!
John, i. 29.

The Shepherd and Bishop of your souls.
1 Peter, ii. 25

The Crook.

HE will redeem our deadly drooping ſtate,
    He will bring home the ſheep that go
        aſtray,
    He will help them that hope in Thee alway,
He will appeaſe our diſcord and debate,
He will ſoon ſave, though we repent us late.
    He will be ours if we continue His,
        He will bring bale to joy and perfeſt bliſs;
He will redeem the flock of His eleſt
                From all that is
                Or was amiſs,
Since Abraham's heirs did firſt His law rejeſt.
                    Geo. Gaſcoigne.

The Lord is my Shepherd, I shall not want. He maketh me to lie down in green pastures; He leadeth me beside the still waters; He restoreth my foul.

Ps. XXIII. 1-3.

Unity.

Ther foundation can no man lay than that which is laid. Upon this then let us build, and as a foundation let us cleave to it as a branch to a vine, and let there be no interval between us and Christ. For if there be any interval, immediately we perish. For so the branch by its adherence draws in the fatness, and the building stands because it is cemented together. All these things indicate Unity, and they allow no void interval, not even the smallest. For he that removes but to a little distance will go on till he has become very far distant. For so the body receiving through it but a small sword=cut perishes; and the building, though there be but a small chink, falls to decay; and the branch, though it be but a little while cut off from the root, becomes useless. So that this trifle is no trifle, but even almost the whole.

St. Chrysostom.

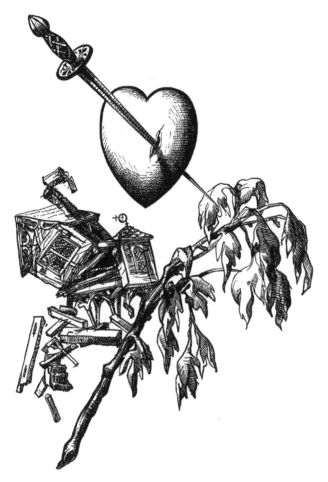

A good foundation againſt the time to come, that they may lay
hold on eternal life.

1 Timothy, vi. 19.

The Gospels.

FOr those blest penmen of Thy Word,
    Who have evangelized of Thee,
We magnify Thy Name, O Lord,
And thankful we desire to be.

The welcome news Thy Gospel brings
With joyful hearts we do embrace,
And prize above all earthly things
That precious earnest of Thy grace.

Enable us to judge and know,
When we new doctrines do receive,
If they agreeing be or no
To what a Christian should believe.

                Geo. Wither.

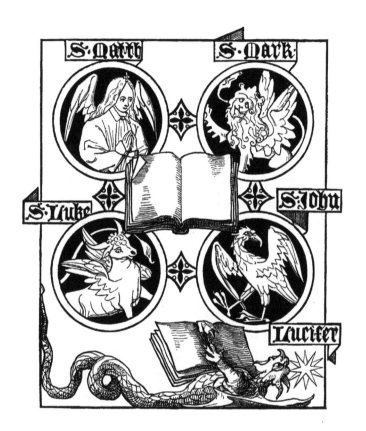

But though we, or an angel from heaven, preach any other gospel unto you than that which we have preached unto you, let him be accursed.

Galatians, 1. 8.

Humility.

He merlin cannot ever soar so high,
   Nor greedy greyhound still pursue the
      chase;
The tender lark will find a time to fly,
And fearful hare to run a quiet race:
He that high growth on cedars did bestow,
Gave also lowly mushrooms leave to grow.

Robert Southwell.

Even so the great and powerful Three in
      One,
That sits upon His all-enlightening throne,
Does not deny to let His mercies crown
The poorest peasant with as much renown
As the most stateliest emperor.

John Quarles.

He forgetteth not the cry of the humble.

Ps. ix. 12.

The Eclipse.

Who can endure the fierce rays of the Sun of Justice? Who shall not be consumed by His beams? Therefore the Sun of Justice took flesh, that, through the conjunction of that Sun and this human body, a shadow may be made.

Guil.

I sat under his shadow with great delight.
Solomon's Song, ii. 3.

Nature.

Who hath adorned the heavens with stars? Who hath stored the air with fowl, the waters with fish, the earth with plants and flowers? But what are all these, but a small spark of divine beauty?

St. Bonaventura.

Let them know how much better the Lord of them is : for the first
Author of beauty hath created them.

Wisdom, xiii. 3.

Light.

Ay, from what golden quivers of the sky
   Do all thy winged arrows fly?
Swiftness and power by birth are thine,
From thy Great Sire they came—thy Sire, the
   Word Divine.

Cowley.

Let there was light be light and there

Genesis, 1. 3.

The Firmament.

When I survey the bright
    Celestial sphere,
So rich with jewels hung, that night
    Doth like an Ethiop bride appear,

My soul her wings doth spread,
    And heavenward flies,
Th' Almighty's mysteries to read,
    In the large volume of the skies.

For the bright firmament
    Shoots forth no flame
So silent, but is eloquent
    In speaking the Creator's name.

                  Wm. Habingdon.

The heavens declare the glory of God.

Ps. xix. 1.

Ornament.

hen lavish art her costly work had done,
The honour and the prize of bravery
Was by the garden from the palace won;
And every rose and lily there did stand
Better attired by Nature's hand:
The case thus judged against the king, we see,
By one that would not be so rich, though wiser
far than he.

Abraham Cowley.

Even Solomon in all his glory was not arrayed
like one of these.

Matt. vi. 29.

God's Gifts.

He gives us this eternal spring,
    Which here enamels everything,
And sends the fowls to us in care,
On daily visits through the air.

He hangs in shades the orange bright,
Like golden lamps in a green night,
And does in the pomegranate close
Jewels more rich than Ormus shows.

He makes the figs our mouths to meet,
And throws the melons at our feet:
With cedars chosen by His hand
From Lebanon He stores the land.

He cast, of which we rather boast,
The gospel's pearl upon our coast,
And in these rocks for us did frame
A temple where to sound His Name.

                              Andrew Marvel.

I muse on the works of Thy hands.

Ps. cxliii. 5.

Chaff and Wheat.

They are the corn, they are in the floor; in the floor they can have the chaff with them; they will not have them in the barn. Let them endure what they would not, that they may come to what they would.

St. Augustine.

He will throughly purge His floor, and gather His wheat into the garner;
but He will burn up the chaff with unquenchable fire.

Matt. iii. 12.

Solitude.

TO "build desolate places" is to banish from the heart's interior the stirrings of earthly desires, and, with a single aim at the eternal inheritance, to pant in love of inward peace. Had he not banished from himself all the risings of the imaginations of the heart, who said, "One thing have I desired of the Lord, that will I seek after, that I may dwell in the House of the Lord?" for he had betaken himself from the concourse of earthly desires to no less a solitude than his own self, where he would be the more secure in seeing nought without, in proportion as there was no insufficient object that he loved. For from the tumult of earthly things he had sought a singular and perfect retreat in a quiet mind, wherein he would see God the more clearly, in proportion as he saw Him alone, with himself also alone.

St. Gregory the Great.

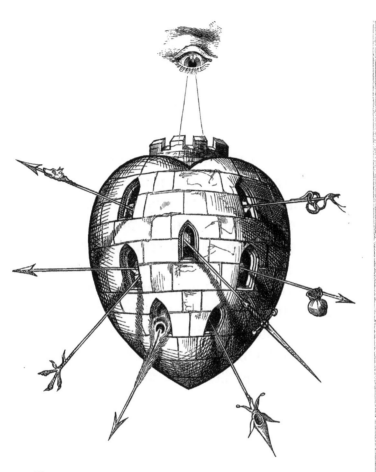

I had been at reſt, with kings and counſellers of the earth, which
built deſolate places for themſelves.

Job, iii, 13, 14,

Experience.

En for the most part, when delivered from shipwreck, renounce thenceforward the ship and the sea, and, by remembering the danger, honour the good gift of God, that is, their own preservation. I commend their fear,—I love their modesty;—they would not a second time be a burden to the divine mercy; they are afraid of seeming to tread under foot that which they have already obtained:—they shun, with assuredly a righteous care, to make trial a second time of that which they have once learned to fear.

Tertullian.

The waters compassed me about, even to the soul: the
depth closed me round about, the weeds were wrapped about
my head.   I went down to the bottoms of the mountains;
the earth with her bars was about me for ever: yet hast
Thou brought up my life from corruption, O Lord my God.

Jonah, ii. 5, 6.

God is All.

God is all to thee:—if thou be hungry, He is bread; if thirsty, He is water; if darknefs, He is light; if naked, He is a Robe of Immortality.

St. Auguftine.

The true 𝔅read from 𝔥eaven. John, vi. 32.

The fountain of the 𝔚ater of life. Rev. xxi. 6.

The Light of the world. John, iv. 10.

A 𝔎obe of righteousness. Isaiah, lxi. 10.

The Law and Gospel.

What wings should I desire, but the two precepts of love on which the Law and the Prophets depend? Oh, if I could obtain these wings, I could fly from Thy face to Thy face, from the face of Thy justice to the face of Thy mercy! Let us find those wings by love, which we have lost by lust.

St. Augustine.

Thou ſhalt love the Lord thy God with all thy heart, and with all thy ſoul, and with all thy mind.

Thou ſhalt love thy neighbour as thyſelf.   On theſe two commandments hang all the law and the prophets.   Matt. xxii. 37, 39, 40.

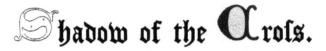 Shadow of the Cross.

Lord, let my soul flee from the scorching thoughts of the world under the covert of Thy wings; that, being refreshed by the moderation of Thy shadow, she may sing merrily, "In peace will I lay me down and rest."

St. Augustine.

I sat down under his shadow with great delight.

Solomon's Song, ii. 3.

The
Altar of our Hearts.

IT is well said to Moses, " The fire on the altar shall always burn which the priest shall feed, putting wood on it every day in the morning." For the Altar of God is our heart, in which the fire is ordered always to burn; because it is necessary that the flame of love should constantly ascend therefrom to God, and the priest should put wood thereon every day left it should go out. For every one who is endowed with faith in Christ, is made specially a member of the Great High Priest, as Peter the Apostle says to all the faithful, " But ye are a chosen race, a royal priesthood."

St. Gregory the Great.

I will offer to Thee the sacrifice of thanksgiving, and will call upon the name of the Lord.

Ps. cxvi. 17.

Impreſs.

Ẁe've nothing but ourſelves, and ſcarce
that neither;
Uile dirt and clay;
Yet it is ſoft and may
Impreſſion take.
Accept it, Lord, and ſay, this Thou hadſt rather;
Stamp it, and on this ſordid metal make
Thy Holy Image, and it ſhall outſhine
The beauty of the golden mine.

Amen.

Jeremy Taylor.

As we have borne the image of the earthy, we shall also bear
the image of the heavenly.

1 Cor. xv. 49.

The Crofs.

Who can blot out the crofs, which th' in-
strument
Of God dewed on me in the Sacrament?
Who can deny me power and liberty
To ftretch mine arms and mine own crofs to be?
Swim, and at every ftroke thou art thy crofs;
The maft and yard make one where feas do tofs;
Look down, thou fpieft out croffes in fmall things;
Look up, thou feeft birds raifed on croffed wings.

Donne.

Both above and below, without and within,
which way foever thou doft turn thee,
everywhere thou fhalt find the crofs.

Thomas à Kempis.

God forbid that I should glory, save in the cross of our Lord
Jesus Christ.

Gal. vi. 14.

Contrast.

HE was crowned with thorns Who crowns martyrs with eternal flowers; He smitten on the face with palms Who yields true palms to them that conquer; He stripped of His earthly raiment Who clothes others with the robe of Immortality; He received gall for food Who gave the food of Heaven; and He had vinegar to drink Who instituted the Cup of Salvation.

St. Cyprian.

The obsequies of Him that could not die,
    And death of life, end of eternity,
How worthily he died, that died unworthily.

Giles Fletcher.

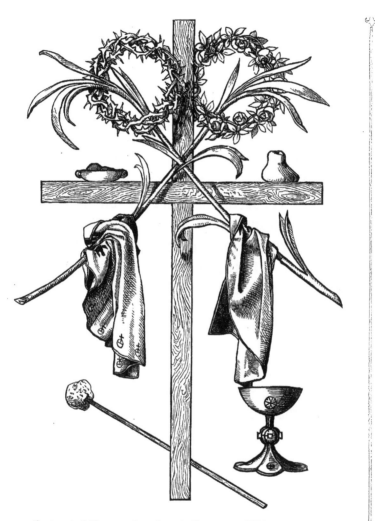

He was despised, and we esteemed him not.   Isaiah, liii. 3.
His glory is above the earth and heaven.   Ps. cxlviii. 13.

Charms of the Cross.

Christ's cross is the christcross of all our happiness; it delivers us from all blindness of error, and enriches our darkness with light; it restoreth the troubled soul to rest; it bringeth strangers to God's acquaintance; it maketh remote foreigners near neighbours; it cutteth off discord, concludeth a league of everlasting peace, and is the bounteous author of all good.

St. Augustine.

In the ✠ is salvation, in the ✠ is life, in the ✠ is protection against our enemies, in the ✠ is infusion of heavenly sweetness, in the ✠ is strength of mind, in the ✠ joy of spirit, in the ✠ the height of virtue, in the ✠ the perfection of sanctity.

Thomas à Kempis.

The beauty of holiness.
1 Chronicles, xvi. 29.

Aspiration.

Whence gathering plumes of perfect specu-
        lation,
To imp the wings of thy high-flying mind,
Mount up aloft through heavenly contemplation
From this dark world, whose damps the soul do
        blind,
And, like the native brood of eagles' kind,
On that bright sun of glory fix thine eyes,
Cleared from gross mists of frail infirmities.

Spenser.

Unto Thee lift I up mine eyes, O Thou that dwellest in the heavens.

Ps. cxxiii. 1.

Excelsior.

When Thou Great Light, whom shepherds
        low adore,
Teach me, O do Thou teach Thy humble swain
To raise my creeping song from earthly floor;
Fill Thou my empty breast with lofty strain,
That, singing of Thy wars and dreadful fight,
My notes may thunder out Thy conquering
        might,
And 'twixt the golden stars cut out her towering
        flight.

                    Phineas Fletcher.

Awake up, my glory; awake, pfaltery and harp.

Ps. lvii. 8.

Faith and Works.

By flowers understand faith; by fruit, good works. As the flower or blossom is before the fruit, so is faith before good works; so neither is the fruit without the flower, nor good works without faith.

St. Bernard.

Faith shall wax strong, and the work shall follow.

2 Esdras, vii. 34.

The
Light of the World.

What darknefs clouds my fenfes? Hath
the day
Forgot his feafon, and the fun his way?
Doth God withdraw His all-fuftaining might,
And works no more with His fair creature—light,
While heaven and earth for fuch, alas! complain,
And turn to rude, unformed heaps again?
My paces with entangling briars are bound,
And all this foreft in deep filence drowned;
Here muft my labour and my journey ceafe,
By which, in vain, I fought for reft and peace;
But now perceive that man's unquiet mind
In all his ways can only darknefs find.
Here muft I ftarve and die unlefs fome light
Point out the paffage from this difmal night.

Sir John Beaumont.

Thou art my lamp, O Lord and the Lord will lighten my darkness.

2 Sam. xxu. 29.

Faith, Hope, Charity.

I Dwell in grace's courts,
    Enriched with virtue's rights;
Faith guides my wit, Love leads my will,
Hope all my mind delights.

Robert Southwell.

OH make us apt to seek and quick to find,
    Thou God most kind!
Give us Love, Hope, and Faith in Thee to trust,
    Thou God most just.

Tho. Heywood.

And now abideth faith, hope, charity, these three.

1 Corinth. xiii. 13.

Calvary.

I Climbed the hill, perufed the crofs,
  Hung with my gain and His great lofs;
Never did tree bear fruit like this,
Balfam of fouls, the body's blifs.

                              Henry Vaughan.

Bleſſed is the wood whereby righteouſneſs cometh.

Wiſdom, xiv. 7.

Crown of Thorns.

Ore wonders did He; for all which suppose
How He was crowned with lily or with rose,
The winding ivy or the glorious bay,
Or myrtle, with the which Uenus, they say,
Girts her proud temples! Shepherds, none of them;
But wore, poor head! a thorny diadem.

                                    Thomas Randolph.

Then came Jesus forth, wearing the crown of thorns.

John, xix. 5.

Christ's Triumph.

YE primroses and purple violets,
    Tell me why blaze ye from your leafy
      beds,
And woo men's hands to rent you from your sets,
As though you would somewhere be carried
With fresh perfumes and velvets garnished;
But ah! I need not ask, 'tis surely so,
You all would to your Saviour's triumph go;
There would ye all await and humble homage do.

              Giles Fletcher.

O grave, where is thy victory?
1 Cor. xv. 55.

Water of Life.

O Precious water, which quencheth the noisome thirst of this world, scoureth all the stains of sinners, that watereth the earth of our souls with heavenly showers, and bringeth back the thirsty heart of man to his only God.

St. Cyril.

And he shewed me a pure river of water of life, clear as crystal, proceeding out of the throne of God and of the Lamb.

Rev. xxii. 1.

Night.

CLouds and thick darknefs are Thy throne,
   Thy wonderful pavilione;
O dart from thence a fhining ray,
And then my midnight fhall be day.

                              Tho. Flatman.

With my foul have I defired Thee in the night.

Ifaiah, xxvi 9.

The Lord my God will enlighten my darknefs.

Ps. xviii. 28.

Dawn.

Rise, sad heart, no longer now withstand;
   Christ's resurrection thine may be;
Do not by hanging down break from the hand
Which, as it riseth, raiseth thee.
                    Arise, arise,
And with His burial-linen dry thine eyes.
Christ left His graveclothes that we might, when
      grief
Draws tears or blood, not want a handkerchief.

Geo. Herbert.

Awake thou that sleepest, and arise from the dead, and Christ
shall give thee light.

Eph. v. 14.

Captivity.

AS on Euphrates' shady banks we lay,
    And there, O Sion, to thy ashes pay
Our funeral tears, our silent harps unstrung
And unregarded on thy willows hung,—
Lo! they who had thy desolation wrought,
And captive Judah unto Babel brought,
Deride the tears which from our sorrows spring,
And say in scorn, " A song of Sion sing."
Shall we profane our harps at their command,
Or holy hymns sing in a foreign land?

Geo. Sandys.

How shall we sing the Lord's song in a strange land?

Ps. cxxxvii. 4.

157

Releafe.

My folk that long in Egypt had been barred,
Whose cries have entered Heaven's
eternal gate,
Our zealous mercy openly hath heard,
Kneeling in tears at our Eternal State.

Mich. Drayton.

With a strong hand hath the Lord brought thee out of Egypt.

Ex. xiii. 9.

The Star.

Bright star, shot from a brighter place,
    Where beams surround my Saviour's
        face,
    Canst thou be anywhere
    So well as there?

Yet if thou wilt from thence depart,
Take a bad lodging in my heart;
    For thou canst make a debtor,
    And make it better.

Sure thou wilt joy by gaining me,
To fly home like a laden bee,
    Unto that hive of beams
    And garland streams.

                    Geo. Herbert.

His glory covered the heavens, and the earth was full of His praise.
And His brightness was as the light.

Habakkuk, iii. 3, 4.

The Soul.

There is nothing to weigh against a soul,
not even the whole world.

> St. Chrysostom.

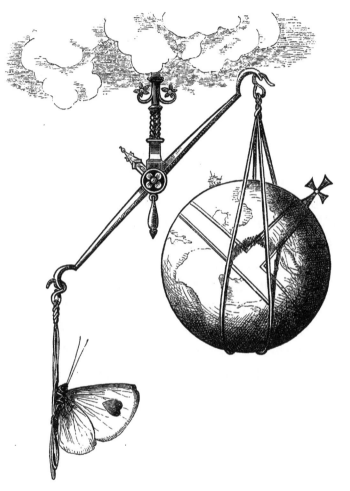

What is a man profited, if he shall gain the whole world, and lose his own soul?

Matt. xvi. 26.

Mutability.

Mutability is the characteristic of things we see. Neither winter nor summer, nor spring nor autumn, is permanent; all are running, flying, and flowing past. Why should I speak of fading flowers, of dignities of kings that are to-day and to-morrow cease to be, of rich men, of magnificent houses, of night and day, of the sun and the moon? for the moon wanes, and the sun is sometimes eclipsed and often darkened with clouds. Of things visible, in short, is there anything that endures for ever? Nothing! no, not anything in us but the soul, and that we neglect.

St. Chrysostom.

He changeth the times and the seasons.

Daniel, ii. 21.

Evanescence.

Look how the flower which lingeringly
        doth fade,
The morning's darling, late the summer's queen,
Spoiled of that juice that kept it fresh and green,
As high as it did raise, bows low the head;
Right so the pleasures of my love being dead,
Or in their contraries but only seen,
With swifter speed declines than erst it spread,
And (blasted) scarce now shows what it hath been.

                                    Wm. Drummond.

All flefh is as grafs.   1 Peter, i. 24.

Ḧe cometh forth like a flower, and is cut down : ḧe fleeth alfo as a fḧadow, and continueth not.

Job, xiv. 2.

Vanity.

Where is he that was clad in raiment of gold? he that rode in the chariot? he that had armies, that had the girdle, that had the heralds? He that was flaying these, and casting those into prison? He that put to death whom he would, and set free whom he was minded? I see nothing but bones, and a worm, and a spider's web; all these things are earth, all these a fable, all a dream, and a shadow, and a bare relation, and a picture, or rather, not so much as a picture. For the picture we see at least is a likeness, but here not so much as a likeness.

St. Chrysostom.

These (all the poor remains of state¹)
    Adorn the rich or praise the great,

Are senseless of the fame they give.

T. Parnell.

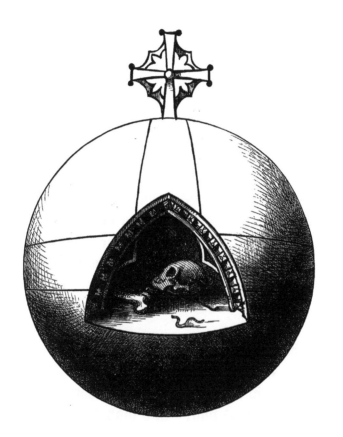

Vanity of vanities; all is vanity.

Ecclesiastes, i. 2.

Sic Vita.

Like to the falling of a star,
  Or as the flights of eagles are,
Or like the fresh Spring's gaudy hue,
Or silver drops of morning dew,
Or like a wind that chafes the flood,
Or bubbles which on water stood:
Even such is man, whose borrowed light
Is straight called in, and paid to-night.

The wind blows out, the bubble dies;
The Spring entombed in Autumn lies;
The dew dries up, the star is shot,
The flight is past,—and man forgot.

Henry King.

For what is your life? It is even a vapour, that appeareth for a
little time, and then vanisheth away.

James, iv. 14.

The Mourning Harp.

For I have seen the pine,
    Famed for its travels o'er the sea,
Broken with storms and age, decline,
    And in some creek unpitied rot away.

I have seen cedars fall,
    And in their room a mushroom grow;
I have seen comets, threatening all,
    Vanish themselves; I have seen princes so.

Vain trivial dust, weak man,
    Where is that virtue of thy breath
That others save or ruin can,
    When thou thyself art called to account by
        death?

When I consider thee,
    The scorn of time and sport of fate,
How can I turn to jollity
    My ill=strung harp, and court the delicate?

                    Wm. Habingdon.

O that they were wise, that they understood this, that they would consider their latter end!

Deuteron. xxxii. 29.

Life and Death.

The time wherein we live is taken from the span of our life; and what remaineth is daily made less, insomuch that the time of our life is nothing but a passage to death.

St. Augustine.

On my eyelids is the shadow of death.
Job, xvi. 16.

Good Life.

IT is not growing like a tree
   In bulk doth make man better be,
Or standing long an oak three hundred year,
To fall a log at last, dry, bald, and sere;
     A lily of a day
     Is fairer far in May;
Although it fall and die that night,
It was the plant and flower of light.
In small proportions we just beauties see,
And in short measure life may perfect be.

Ben Jonson.

Honourable age is not that which standeth in length of time, nor that is measured by number of years.

Wisdom, iv. 8.

Weak and Strong.

For God's fake mark that fly,
   See what a poor weak little thing it is!
When thou haft marked and fcorned it, know
     that this,
   This little, poor, weak fly
Has killed a pope, can make an emperor die.

   Behold yon fpark of fire,
How little hot, how near to nothing 'tis!
When thou haft done defpifing, know that this,
   This contemn'd fpark of fire,
Has burnt whole towns, can burn a world entire.

   That crawling worm there fee,
Ponder how ugly, filthy, vile is he!
When thou haft feen and loathed it know that this,
   This bafe worm thou doft fee,
Has quite devoured thy parents, fhall eat thee.

   Honour, the world, and man,
What trifles are they! fince moft true it is
That this poor fly, this fmall fpark, this
   So much abhorr'd worm can
Honour deftroy—burn worlds—devour up man.
              Patrick Carey.

Behold, how great a matter a little fire kindleth!

James, iii. 5.

Shortcomings of Earth.

Such is the weaknes of all mortal hope;
    So tickle is the ſtate of earthly things,
That, ere they come into their aimed ſcope,
They fall too ſhort of our frail reckonings,
And bring us bale and bitter ſorrowings,
Inſtead of comfort, which we ſhould embrace.
This is the ſtate of keaſars and of kings:
Let none, therefore, that is in meaner place,
Too greatly grieve at any his unlucky caſe.

                                    Edmund Spenſer.

The things which are seen are temporal.

2 Cor. iv. 18.

Daffodils.

Fair daffodils, we weep to see
    You haste away so soon;
As yet the early rising sun
Has not attained his noon.
      Stay, stay,
Until the lasting day
      Has run
But to the even-song:
And, having prayed together, we
    Will go with you along.

Robert Herrick.

The flower fadeth, becaufe the fpirit of the Lord bloweth upon it :
furely the people is grafs.

Ifaiah, xl. 7.

Farewell! World!

Farewell, ye gilded follies, pleasing troubles!
Farewell, ye honoured rags, ye glorious bubbles!
Fame's but a hollow echo; gold, pure clay;
Honour, the darling but of one short day;
Beauty, th' eye's idol, a damasked skin;
State, but a golden prison to live in,
And torture free-born minds; embroidered trains,
Merely but pageants for proud swelling veins;
And blood allied to greatness is alone
Inherited, not purchased, not our own:
Fame, honour, beauty, state, train, blood, and birth,
Are but the fading blossoms of the earth.

Sir Henry Wotton.

The land shall be utterly emptied, and utterly spoiled: for the Lord hath spoken this word. The earth mourneth and fadeth away, the world languisheth and fadeth away, the haughty people of the earth do languish.

Isaiah, xxiv. 3, 4.

b b

Viciſſitude.

The lopped tree in time may grow again,
 Moſt naked plants renew both fruit and
  flower,
The ſorrieſt wight may find releaſe of pain,
The drieſt ſoil ſuck in ſome moiſtening ſhower;
Time goes by turns, and chances change by
  courſe,
From foul to fair, from better hap to worſe.

Robert Southwell.

I am full of toſſings to and fro.

Job, vii. 4.

Sabbath.

Thou art a day of mirth,
 And where the week=days trail on ground
Thy flight is higher, as thy birth;
O let me take thee at the bound,
Leaping with thee from seven to seven,
Till that we both, being tossed from earth,
 Fly hand in hand to heaven.

Geo. Herbert.

My presence shall go with thee, and I will give thee rest.

Exodus, xxxiii. 14.

Affliction.

Ake well whate'er shall chance, though
bad it be,
Take it for good and 'twill be good to thee.

Tho. Randolph.

Weet are the uses of adversity,
Which, like the toad, ugly and venomous,
Yet wears a precious jewel in its head.

Shakespeare.

Whom the Lord loveth he chasteneth.
Heb. xii. 6.

Bitter Sweet.

AND juſt as the roots of tears are bitter, and yet they produce our ſweeteſt fruits; ſo verily godly ſorrow will bring us an abundant pleaſure. They know, who have often prayed with anguiſh and ſhed tears, what gladneſs they have reaped; how they purged the conſcience; how they roſe up with favourable hopes.

St. Chryſoſtom.

They that sow in tears shall reap in joy.

Ps. cxxvi. 5.

The Fight.

IF there be no enemy, no fight; if no fight, no victory; if no victory, no crown.

Savanarola.

BE thou therefore prepared for the fight, if thou wilt have the victory.

Thomas à Kempis.

Fight the good fight of faith.
1 Tim. vi. 12.

ribulation.

hou must pass through fire and water before thou come to the place of refreshing.

Thomas à Kempis.

So he bringeth them unto their desired haven.

Ps. cvii. 30.

197

Glory.

Et us suffer with those that suffer, and be crucified with those that be crucified, that we may be glorified with those that are glorified.

Macarius.

Suffer with Christ and for Christ, if thou desire to reign with Christ.

Thomas à Kempis.

Be thou faithful unto death, and I will give thee a crown of life.
Rev. ii. 10.

Hymn.

My joy, my life, my crown.
My heart was meaning all the day,
Something it fain would say;
And still it runneth mutt'ring up and down
With only this,
My joy, my life, my crown.

G. Herbert.

Thanks be to God, which giveth us the victory through
our Lord Jesus Christ.

1 Cor. xv. 57.

Ambrose (St.)

His distinguished prelate was born at Arles, A. D. 340, and, after having been for five years governor, was elected bishop of Milan. His vigorous denunciation of wrong is historically important, as having subdued the haughty spirit of the Emperor Theodosius. St. Ambrose died at Milan, A. D. 397.

P. 44.

Anselm,

He founder of logic, and one of the most learned writers of the 11th century, was born at Aosta, Piedmont, A. D. 1033, and, on coming to England, became Archbishop of Canterbury in the reign of William Rufus. He was the first to perceive and inculcate the value of Natural Theology. He died at Canterbury, A. D. 1109.

P. 6.

203

Augustine (St.),

ISHOP of Hippo, was born at Tagaste, in Africa, A. D. 354. This learned and acute father of the Church wrote voluminously against sectarian tendencies, and his pious and practical sermons warrant the high rank he holds in ecclesiastical literature. The date of his death is uncertain.

Pp. 2, 8, 32, 78, 84, 112, 118, 120, 122, 132, 174.

Beaumont (Sir John),

ROTHER of Francis Beaumont, the poetical associate of Fletcher, was born A. D. 1584, became judge under Queen Elizabeth, wrote a volume of sacred poetry, and died, A. D. 1628, after having been knighted by Charles I.

P. 140.

Bernard (St.)

HIS religious writer was, in the 12th century, Abbot of Clairval. He was the great ecclesiastical champion of the Crusades, and the vigorous opponent of the doctrine of the Immaculate Conception of the Virgin Mary. He died A. D. 1153.

Pp. 60, 138.

Bonaventura.

A Writer on philosophical theology, whose works have been classed with those of Albertus Magnus and Thomas Aquinas. An incidental interest attaches to his name in the fact of his having been the friend of Petrarch. He was born at Padua in the first half of the 14th century, and suffered a violent death, A.D. 1386.

P. 102.

Bunyan (John),

The author of England's great "Puritan Epic," the Pilgrim's Progress, was the son of a travelling tinker. He became a preacher at Bedford, where, in confinement for his religious opinions, he composed his immortal work. He was born A.D. 1628, and died A.D. 1688.

P. 30.

Carew (Thomas).

Born A.D. 1577, died A.D. 1639. This poet received his education at Corpus Christi College, Oxford. He was elevated to the post of Gentleman of the Privy Chamber by Charles I. and his "Masques" were well received at court.

P. 82.

Carey (Patrick).

TO Sir Walter Scott is due the honour of first making the public acquainted with the poems of Patrick Carey. Little is known of him, except that he was an English churchman and loyalist. The MS. poems which Sir Walter edited bear the date A. D. 1651.

P. 178.

Chrysostom (St.)

IOhannes Secundus, commonly known by the title of St. Chrysostom, from his eloquence, was a native of Antioch, and shortly after his ordination was raised to the patriarchate of Constantinople. His popularity however was fruitful of jealousy, and the patriarch was deposed, and eventually banished by the Empress Eudoxia. He died A D. 407. His sermons, happily preserved, abound in devotional thought and original exposition.

Pp. 10, 24, 30, 38, 40, 42, 54, 56, 62, 70, 76, 94, 162, 164, 168, 192.

Cowley (Abraham).

THis quaint poet was born A. D. 1618. On leaving Westminster School he went first to Cambridge, then to Oxford, and afterwards to France. He was a most zealous loyalist, and assisted Queen Henrietta Maria in corresponding with her Royal Consort. At the Restoration he received a grant of property at Chertsey, where he died, A. D. 1667.

Pp. 104, 108.

Crashaw (Richard).

The date of this author's birth is uncertain. He was educated at the Charter-house and took his degree at Cambridge. After embracing the Roman faith he repaired to Italy, where he died, A. D. 1650. He was a personal friend of Cowley. Coleridge was a great admirer of his poetry.

P. 86.

Cyprian (St.),

Bishop of Carthage in the 3rd century, was the successor of Donatus, during the reign of the Emperor Decius Trajan. He successfully argued that those who had deserted the church through fear of martyrdom could not without penance be readmitted within its pale. He was the author of a volume of epistles, and suffered martyrdom, A. D. 258.

Pp. 4, 130.

Cyril (St.)

Bishop of Jerusalem in the 4th century, and the author of some discourses delivered in that city.

P. 150.

Davies (Sir John),

BOrn A.D. 1570, received his education at Oxford. He was knighted on the accession of King James I. and was eventually raised to the office of Chief Justice of the King's Bench. His death occurred A.D. 1626. His principal work, a noble poem on the Immortality of the Soul, is full of vigorous thought and poetical treatment.

P. 68.

Dekker (Thomas).

ONe of the Elizabethan dramatists, of whose life but little is known. The chief event in his history which has come down to us is his violent quarrel with Ben Jonson. Dekker's most noted performance is the drama of " Old Fortunatus."

P. 12.

Donne (John),

THe " Founder of the Metaphysical School of Poetry," as he has been termed by Dr. Johnson, was born in London, A.D. 1573. His early works had little of serious sentiment, but his talents flowed into a genuine religious channel after his ordination. He became Dean of St. Paul's, and died A.D. 1631, leaving a crowd of enthusiastic admirers.

Pp. 26, 128.

Drayton (Michael).

Born at Harshall in Warwickshire A.D. 1563, and educated at Orford. In youth he was a page; in after life he obtained the friendship and patronage of the wealthy and high-born, and became Poet Laureate of England. He died A.D. 1631.

Pp. 56, 158.

Drummond (William).

Drummond of Hawthornden, the son of Sir John Drummond, was born A.D. 1585. Abandoning the profession of the law, which he had embraced, he retired to his Scottish estate, and passed his life in the poetical enjoyment of literary leisure. He died, A.D. 1649, of grief occasioned by the execution of King Charles I.

Pp. 50, 166.

Ephrem (St.)

St. Ephrem or St. Ephraim, the Syrian, was one of the most poetical and devotional writers of the 4th century. He is principally remarkable for his attacks on heretical doctrine and his elucidations of the Sacred Word.

P. 34.

Flatman.

This variously esteemed writer was born A.D. 1633. He was often pleasing, although never sublime. He died A.D. 1688.

P. 152.

Fletcher (Giles).

He was born A.D. 1588, and having been presented to the living of Alderton, Suffolk, died there, A.D. 1623. He never wrote a vulgar line, or a verse destitute of the sweetest manly piety.

Pp 6, 20, 34, 130, 148.

Fletcher (Phineas).

A.D. 1584 was born the remarkable author of "The Purple Island." It is a noble composition, descriptive, in Spenserian verse, of the physical and moral constitution of man. Phineas Fletcher, who was the elder brother of the foregoing, held the living of Hilgay, in Norfolk, for twenty-nine years, and died circa A.D. 1650.

P. 136

Gascoigne (George),

AN early English poet, born A.D. 1540. He was the son of Sir John Gascoigne, studied at Cambridge, and afterwards repaired to Holland, where he held a commission under the Prince of Orange. For the period in which he lived his verses are unusually melodious. He died A.D. 1577.

Pp. 84, 92.

Gregory of Nyssa (St.),

BISHOP of Nyssa A.D. 372, and one of the most powerful supporters of the doctrine of the Holy Trinity. He drew up the Nicene creed at the council of Constantinople, and died A D. 396.

P. 58.

Gregory the Great (St.)

THIS famous ecclesiastic was born during the first half of the 6th century in Rome. Although the author of epistles and dialogues, he is chiefly known as the great patron of Augustine's Christian mission to England. He was a man of most opposite qualities; to an unbounded zeal for the cause of truth he united a superstitious reverence for worthless forms, and his noblest intentions were often stultified by the introduction of pitiful details. He died A.D. 604

Pp. 14, 36, 114, 124.

Gulielmus.

William of Rheims, a devout writer of the 12th century whose works abound in practical piety, for the most part untinged with the eccentric minutiæ common to the productions of his contemporaries.

P. 100.

Habington (William).

This poet was born at Hendlip in Worcestershire, A.D. 1605. He was educated in France, married Lucia, daughter of Herbert, first Lord Powis, and died A.D. 1654. He published a volume of poems which he entitled "Castara," a drama, and some prose dissertations.

Pp. 106, 172.

Herbert (George).

This most celebrated of all English poetical divines was born at Montgomery Castle, in Wales, A.D. 1593. He was a scion of the noble house of Pembroke, and became Rector of Bemerton, near Salisbury, where he died, A.D. 1632.

Pp. 46, 88, 154, 160, 188, 200.

Herrick (Robert).

This sprightly writer was born in London, A.D. 1591. Most of his poems glow with genial good-humour and sterling sense. He was presented by King Charles I. to the vicarage of Dean Prior, in Devonshire.

P. 182.

Heywood (Thomas).

This voluminous Elizabethan poet devoted his talents chiefly to dramatic works, but he also wrote, circa A.D. 1635, "The Hierarchies of the blessed Angels," and other poems. The dates of his birth and death are not precisely recorded, nor are all his writings extant.

P. 142.

Hugo (Herman),

A Latin theological writer and poet, who was born in Belgium, A.D. 1588, and died at Rhinberg, A.D. 1629.

Pp. 46, 48.

Jonſon (Ben).

THis famous dramatic poet paſſed a chequered and eventful life; at one time working as a bricklayer, at another thrown into priſon for duelling, at another honoured by the title of Poet Laureate and penſioned by the court. He was the friend of Shakeſpeare. Ben Jonſon was born A.D. 1574, died A.D. 1637, and was buried in Weſtminſter Abbey. His laconic epitaph, "O rare Ben Jonſon," has almoſt paſſed into a proverb.

P. 176.

Kempis (Thomas à).

THis popular writer was born in the dioceſe of Cologne, A.D. 1380. His great book, "The Imitation of Chriſt," is too well known throughout Chriſtendom to require any deſcription. He died A.D. 1471.

Pp. 14, 128, 132, 194, 196, 198.

King (Henry),

BOrn A.D. 1591. He was a writer who diſplayed in his poems much of the quaint thought of the Elizabethan era, conveyed in particularly harmonious verſe. He died, A.D. 1669, in the poſition of Biſhop of Chicheſter.

P. 170.

Lyndſay (Sir David).

Hiſ Scottiſh poet was born at Garmylton, Haddingtonſhire, A.D. 1490. He, while page to the young King James U. compoſed the poems, "The Dream," and "The Complaint," and was ſubſequently ſent on a miſſion to the Emperor Charles U. His tendencies were ſtrongly in favour of the Reformed Church. He died A.D. 1557.

P. 24.

Macarius.

An Egyptian eccleſiaſtic of the 4th century, whoſe glowing pictures of the charms of a religious life have given him a high ſtanding among early Chriſtian writers. Having been baniſhed to an iſland, he converted its inhabitants to the faith, and died A.D. 395.

P. 198.

Marvell (Andrew),

Born at Hull, A.D. 1620, and educated at Cambridge, received the appointment of ſecretary to the Engliſh Embaſſy at Conſtantinople. He is ſaid to have aſſiſted Milton as Latin ſecretary to Oliver Cromwell. After the Reſtoration he became member for his native town, and was often tempted, but in vain, by offers of lucrative employment, to abandon his ſtern political principles. His poetry is warm and graceful, but he was not a voluminous writer. Marvell died A.D. 1678.

P. 110.

M. S.

The ancient English poem, from which an extract is here given, forms part of a manuscript in the Bodleian Library (Digby, No. 86, fol. 163). The poem is of the time of Edward I. and is entitled by Mr. Wright, who has printed it in his "Anecdota Literaria," "Song on the Uncertainty of Worldly Affairs." It has a higher tone of morality and of poetical feeling than most contemporary productions in the English language.

P. 52.

Milton (John),

The immortal author of "Paradise Lost" and "Lycidas," was born A. D. 1608, and died A. D. 1674.

Pp. 48, 80.

More (Henry).

This poet and philosopher was born at Grantham, in Lincolnshire, A D. 1614, and became Prebend of Gloucester, refusing any higher promotion. He died A. D. 1687.

P. 16.

Nazianzen (St. Gregory),

ON of the Bishop of Nazianzum in Cappadocia, and a friend of St. Basil, was born A.D. 324. He was elected Bishop of Constantinople, A.D. 380. He has obtained a very honourable position among the theological writers of his era for the gracefulness and purity of his style. His death took place A.D. 389.

P. 22.

Norris (John).

BEmerton Rectory, after having been rendered illustrious by the occupancy of George Herbert, was destined to be connected with the name of another English poet, the Rev. J. Norris. He was born A.D. 1657, and produced a number of writings both in prose and verse. He died at Bemerton, A.D. 1711.

P. 28.

Parnell (Thomas).

This author was born in Dublin, A.D. 1679. He held the position of Archdeacon of Clogher, and was the friend both of Pope and Swift. A.D. 1717 he died at Chester, on his journey from London to his native city.

P. 168.

Quarles (Francis).

The author of "Quarles' Emblems," a work which has gone through a vast number of editions, was born A.D. 1592, at Stewards, near Romford, Essex. He was educated at Christ's College, Cambridge, and afterwards became cupbearer to Elizabeth of Bohemia, daughter of James I. The chief part of his life was, however, spent in literary retirement. His loyalty to Charles I. brought him into disgrace with the parliament, and he died A.D. 1644, after the sequestration of his property and papers.

Pp. 48, 50, 66, 72.

Quarles (John),

The son of Francis Quarles, was born A.D. 1624. He was the author of many poetical works, all of a religious character. He died of the plague, A.D. 1665.

P. 98.

Randolph (Thomas).

This poet was the adopted son of Ben Jonson. He was born A.D. 1605, and died A.D. 1634. His compositions took for the most part a dramatic form.

Pp. 146, 190.

Sandys (George),

SEcond son of Archbishop Sandys of York, was born at Bishop's-Thorpe, A.D. 1587, and educated at Oxford. Much of his time was spent abroad, and on his return to England he published an account of his travels. His best works are paraphrases of Holy Scripture. He died A.D. 1643.

P. 156.

Savanarola (Jerome).

THis devout precursor of the Reformation was born at Ferrara, A.D. 1452, and became a Dominican. His enthusiastic denunciation, however, of the corruptions and abuses of the Church of Rome brought down upon him the vengeance of the papal authorities, and he was committed to the flames at Florence, A.D. 1498, bearing his fate with fortitude and resignation. His chief production is "The Triumph of the Cross."

P. 194.

Shakespeare (William).

DRamatic poet. Born A.D. 1564, died A.D. 1616.

P. 190.

Sherburne (Sir Edward),

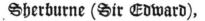

A Catholic poet and an enthusiastic loyalist. He held an official post under Charles I. and after the Restoration was knighted by Charles II. His attachment to James II. occasioned a reverse of his fortunes, and he died in poverty, A. D. 1702.

P. 64.

Southwell (Robert).

This little-known poet was born at St. Faith's, Norfolk, A. D. 1560. He was a Roman Catholic, and was executed at Tyburn, A. D. 1595.

Pp. 98, 142, 186.

Spenser (Edmund).

This masterly poet was born in London circa A. D. 1553, and educated at Pembroke Hall, Cambridge. His great work, "The Faerie Queene," is one of the finest poems in the English language. Spenser was patronized by Queen Elizabeth and her court, and received the grant of an estate in Ireland. He died in London of a broken heart, A. D. 1599, and was buried in Westminster Abbey by the Earl of Essex.

Pp. 90, 134, 180.

Taylor (Jeremy),

The most illustrious of English preachers, was born at Cambridge, A. D. 1613. His prose works are all of the noblest order, and his few hymns and poems, vigorous and devotional. He was Chaplain to Charles I. was twice imprisoned during the Commonwealth, and after the Restoration advanced to the Bishopric of Down and Connor. He died A. D. 1667.

P. 126.

Tertullian (Quintus S. F.)

This early defender of Christianity was by birth a Carthaginian. He was learned and eloquent, and devoted his genius chiefly to vindicating the doctrines of Christianity in the reign of the Emperor Severus. His "Treatise against the Jews" is open to many objections; but his "Apology for the Christians," by which he is best known, has always been highly esteemed. He died circa A. D. 245.

P. 116.

Vaughan (Henry).

An accomplished poet, born at Newton, in Brecknockshire, A. D. 1621. His works are distinguished by fine imagination and devotional feeling. He died A. D. 1695.

P. 144.

Waller (Edmund),

AN elegant and melodious poet of the troublous times of the Civil Wars, was born, A.D. 1605, at Coleshill, Herts, and educated at Cambridge. Unfortunately for his credit he alike flattered Charles I. Oliver Cromwell, Charles II. and James II. as fortune seemed to favour him. He died at Beaconsfield, A.D. 1687.

P. 74.

Wither (George),

WAs born at Brentworth, near Alton, in Hampshire, A.D. 1588, and there are few writers whose poems have been more variously esteemed. He produced a great number of works, both political and religious; the most noted being "Abuses Stript and Whipt," and "Emblems." He died A.D. 1667.

Pp. 18, 96.

Wotton (Sir Henry).

THis versatile writer was born at Boughton Hall, Kent, A.D. 1568. He was variously employed, both by Elizabeth and James I. His prose works are for the most part of a political character, although some are dedicated to religion; his poems are peculiarly sweet and noble. He died A.D. 1640.

P. 184.

The End

Lightning Source UK Ltd.
Milton Keynes UK
UKHW022020090119

335262UK00010B/671/P

9 781527 884540